Wildlife Watching

Eagle Watching

by Diane Bair and Pamela Wright

CAPSTONE BOOKS

an imprint of Capstone Press
Mankato, Minnesota

Capstone Books are published by Capstone Press
151 Good Counsel Drive, P.O. Box 669, Mankato, Minnesota 56002
http://www.capstone-press.com

Library of Congress Cataloging-in-Publication Data
Bair, Diane.
    Eagle watching/by Diane Bair and Pamela Wright.
    p. cm.—(Wildlife watching)
    Includes bibliographical references and index.
    Summary: Describes the physical characteristics, habits, and natural environment
of eagles, the two North American species, and how to safely observe these birds in
the wild.
    ISBN 0-7368-0322-X
    1. Eagles—Juvenile literature. 2. Bird watching—Juvenile literature. [1. Eagles.
2. Bird watching.] I. Wright, Pamela, 1953– . II. Title. III. Series: Bair, Diane.
Wildlife watching.
QL696.F32B338 2000
598.9'42—dc21   99-22956
                                                                                        CIP

Editorial Credits
Matt Doeden, editor; Steve Christensen, cover designer and illustrator; Heidi Schoof,
    photo researcher

Photo Credits
Cheryl A. Ertelt, 7
Colephoto/E. C. Talik, 30; Phyllis Greenberg, 41
David F. Clobes, 4, 14, 20, 32, 38
International Stock/Mark Newman, 12
Photo Network/Mark Newman, 26
Robert McCaw, 11
Root Resources, 37, 44; Root Resources/Alan G. Nelson, 22; Stan Osolinski, 29
Thomas Kitchin/TOM STACK & ASSOCIATES, cover inset, 40
Visuals Unlimited/Arthur Morris, cover, 17, 18; Francis Caldwell, 8; David M.
    Ellie, 34; Ernest Manewal, 47

**Thank you to Christi Hall, The Peregrine Fund, for her assistance in preparing
this book.**

Table of Contents

Chapter 1

Getting to Know Eagles

Many people think of eagles as symbols of freedom. The bald eagle is the national bird of the United States. Some American Indians believe eagles are sacred birds. These American Indians believe the birds are symbols of courage and power.

About Eagles

Eagles are large and powerful birds. They are among the largest birds in North America. Eagles can measure more than 3 feet (.9 meter) from beak to tail. Their wingspans can measure

The bald eagle is the national bird of the United States.

up to 90 inches (229 centimeters). Wingspan is the distance between the tips of a bird's wings.

Eagles are raptors. Raptors are birds that hunt and eat prey. Animals that are hunted by other animals for food are called prey. Raptors have feet with sharp claws called talons. They use their talons to grasp and kill prey. Raptors also have strong, sharp beaks. They use their beaks to tear apart prey. Other raptors include hawks, vultures, and owls.

Eagle Abilities

Eagles have excellent eyesight. They have binocular vision. Binocular vision allows eagles to see distant objects clearly. This helps eagles spot prey while they are flying high in the air.

Eagles' eyes can move separately. One eye can look to the left while the other eye looks to the right. This gives eagles a wide field of vision. Eagles can see more of the area around them than you can.

Eagles have strong, sharp beaks.

Eagles dive to catch prey.

Eagles fly fast. They can fly as fast as 75 miles (121 kilometers) per hour. They fly even faster when they dive for prey. Eagles can reach speeds of 200 miles (322 kilometers) per hour when they dive. This speed allows them to capture their prey by surprise.

Bald eagles can swim. They use their large wings to paddle. Eagles may dive to catch fish.

They sometimes catch fish that are too heavy to carry in the air. The eagles then hold the fish with their talons and swim to shore.

Dangers to Eagles

Eagle populations are smaller today than they were in the past. This is because people have destroyed many eagle habitats by cutting down forests. Habitats are the natural places and conditions in which eagles live. But eagle populations have been rising in recent years. This is because of laws that protect eagles.

People also harm eagles with certain pesticides. People use these chemicals to kill pests such as insects. Farmers often spray pesticides on crops. But some pesticides also harm animals and birds. Eagles may eat prey poisoned by pesticides. The poisons may harm or kill these eagles. The poisons prevent some eagles from producing young.

Today, eagles are protected by laws in the United States and Canada. Governments try to keep eagle habitats safe. Some laws prevent people from using certain harmful pesticides. Laws also prevent people from hunting eagles.

Eagles are important to their habitats. They kill and eat rodents, reptiles, insects, and other animals. This helps keep animal populations in balance. Eagles sometimes eat carrion. Carrion is the flesh of dead animals. This helps to keep eagle habitats clean.

Some scientists believe that eagles are environmental indicators. These scientists believe eagles give people clues about the condition of an area's environment. Areas where you see many eagles often have healthy environments. Areas where eagles are sick and dying may have polluted and unhealthy environments.

Young eagles need environments that are free from pesticides.

Tail:
Eagles use their tail feathers to steer while in flight. They also use these feathers to control the rates at which they rise and fall.

Talons:
Eagles have sharp talons on their toes. These talons grasp and kill prey. Eagles can fly several miles while holding prey in their talons.

Wings:
Eagles have powerful wings. They can fly as fast as 75 miles (121 kilometers) per hour. Their wingspans can be 90 inches (229 centimeters) wide.

Eyes:
Eagles have excellent vision. They can see up to three times better than a person. Eagles can see small prey from a mile away.

Beak:
Eagles' beaks are long and hooked. They also are sharp. Eagles tear meat with their beaks.

Chapter 2

Preparing for Your Adventure

Learn about eagles before you go eagle watching. You are more likely to see eagles if you know where and how they live. Check out books about eagles from your school or local library. Write your state wildlife agency for free information on eagles and eagle watching. You can find this address by searching in phone books and on the Internet.

Study field guides before you go eagle watching. Field guides are books that show what animals look like and tell where they live. Eagles may be included in field guides

You can read books about eagles before you go eagle watching.

on birds of prey, raptors, or North American birds. Carefully study the pictures in these books. This will help you to recognize any eagles you see.

Finding Eagles

Find out if eagles live near your area. Call a local bird-watching group, nature center, or nature park. You can find phone numbers for these places in phone books or on the Internet. Ask if there are eagles nesting or feeding nearby. Ask for directions to good eagle-watching spots.

Find safe, public areas to watch eagles. Do not go to places where there are no roads or trails. Do not go onto private property. People may become angry with you if you go onto their property without permission. State and national wildlife parks are among the best places to look for eagles.

Some state and national wildlife parks offer eagle-watching hikes. Beginning eagle

Study field guides before you go eagle watching. These books will show you how to recognize eagles.

watchers may want to take these hikes. The people who lead the hikes know where to find eagles. They can teach you about eagle habits. They also can give you tips on how to spot eagles.

Binoculars make distant objects appear closer.

What to Bring

Binoculars are one of the most important pieces of eagle-watching equipment. This tool makes distant objects appear closer.

Practice using binoculars before your trip. Learn how to aim them at distant objects. Practice focusing them on different objects.

You can practice in your yard or in a park. Use the binoculars to watch common birds that live near your home.

Bring a field guide on your trip. This will help you identify the eagles and other animals you see. You can check out field guides at most libraries. Many book stores sell inexpensive field guides. A brief field guide begins on page 40 of this book.

Bring materials to record your adventure. A camera with a telephoto lens allows you to take photographs. Telephoto lenses make distant objects appear closer. You also can bring a video camera to take videos of the eagles you see. Bring paper and pencils to take notes and draw pictures.

Safety

Never go eagle watching by yourself. You could get lost or hurt. Watch eagles in groups of two or more. Every eagle-watching group should include at least one adult.

Wear long pants and long-sleeved shirts when you go eagle watching. Tuck your pants into your boots or shoes if you can. This protects you from insect bites. You may want to wear insect repellent during summer. These sprays and lotions help keep many insects away from you.

Dress warmly if you go eagle watching during winter. Wear gloves or mittens to protect your hands. Wear a hat or hood to protect your head. Boots and warm socks will help keep your feet warm.

Be extra careful if you go eagle watching during a hunting season. Many people hunt near eagle habitats. Contact local wildlife agencies to learn when hunting seasons take place. Wear bright colors such as blaze orange if you go eagle watching during hunting seasons. Hunters can see bright colors easily.

Wear pants and long-sleeved shirts when you go eagle watching. This will protect you from insect bites.

Chapter 3

Where to Look

Two kinds of eagles live in North America. They are golden eagles and bald eagles. Each kind of eagle is called a species. Look for each eagle species in its range. A range is the geographic region where a plant or animal species naturally lives. Golden eagles live mainly in the western parts of the United States and Canada. Bald eagles live throughout North America. Bald eagles are most common in Alaska.

Eagle Homes
Eagles usually live near open water. Wide rivers and lakes are common eagle habitats.

Eagles usually live near open water.

23

Places to See Eagles

1 **Chilkat River, Alaska:**
Every fall, thousands of bald eagles gather near the Chilkat River in southeast Alaska. This is the largest gathering of bald eagles in the world. The eagles feed on salmon that swim in the river. As many as 4,000 eagles visit the Chilkat River each year. People have seen up to 20 bald eagles in a single tree.

2 **The Klamath Basin Wildlife Refuges:**
During winter, bald eagles gather at the Klamath Basin Wildlife Refuges along the border between Oregon and California. A refuge is a safe place for animals and birds to feed and nest. The eagles feed on fish and other birds there.

3 **Acadia National Park, Maine:**
There are more than 50 bald eagle nests in Maine's Acadia National Park. The park includes many rocky cliffs along the Atlantic Ocean coastline. During summers, visitors to the park take boat rides to see eagle nests.

4 **Table Rock Lake, Missouri:**
Bald eagles gather along the shores of this lake near Branson, Missouri each winter. The eagles live in the tall bluffs that overlook the lake. Some golden eagles also live in the area.

5 **Goldstream Provincial Park, British Columbia, Canada:**
Thousands of bald eagles gather in this park each winter. Park officials conduct special presentations and activities for eagle watchers.

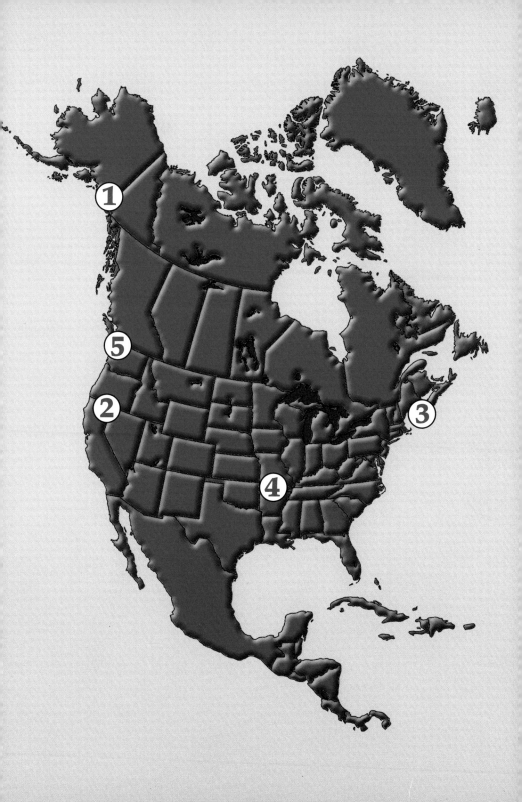

Some eagles live along ocean shores. Eagles hunt for fish and other animals that live in and around water.

Eagles live in roosts. These places are where eagles build nests and raise their young. Eagles build roosts in high places. They do this to stay safe from other animals. Tall trees and mountain cliffs are common places for eagles' roosts.

Eagle Perches and Nests

You usually have to look up to see eagles. They spend much of their time hunting for food. They may fly high in the air to spot prey. Watch the sky for large birds with wide wingspans.

You may spot eagles standing on perches. Tree tops are common eagle perches. Look at the tallest trees in an area. Search for light-colored spots near the tops of the trees. Some eagles have perches on mountain cliffs and ledges. Look for dark spots on open

Watch the sky for large birds with wide wingspans.

mountain ledges. Use binoculars to find out if these spots are eagles.

Look for eagle nests in the tops of the largest trees near a river or lake. Eagles build their nests out of sticks and twigs. Many eagle nests are easy to spot because they can be very large. This is because eagles use the same nests every year. They add sticks and twigs to the nests each year. Large eagle nests can be 6 feet (2 meters) wide and 5 feet (1.5 meters) deep. These nests can weigh as much as a small car.

Eagles built the largest bird nest ever found. It measured 20 feet (6 meters) deep and almost 10 feet (3 meters) across. It weighed more than 2 tons (1.8 metric tons).

Eagles build large nests out of sticks and twigs.

Chapter 4

Making Observations

Be quiet and still while you look for eagles. Eagles may leave an area if you make too much noise or move around too much. Do not get too close to the eagles you see. They may fly away if they sense danger.

Markings

Eagles have markings. Look for these special colors on any large birds you see. Markings will help you identify eagles.

Adult bald eagles have dark brown bodies. Their heads and tails are white. Their beaks, feet, and eyes are yellow. Young bald eagles

Adult bald eagles have white heads.

Golden eagles have gold-colored feathers on the backs of their heads and necks.

are mostly brown with only a few streaks of white on their bodies. Bald eagles' heads and tails may not turn white until they are 4 or 5 years old.

Golden eagles look much like young bald eagles. They are mostly dark brown. But they have gold-colored feathers on the backs of their heads and necks. These feathers give golden eagles their name. Golden eagles have light gray beaks and yellow feet. They have brown tails with scattered patches of white.

Soaring Eagles

Look in the sky for large birds that seem to be floating in the air. Eagles usually fly by gliding along air currents. They hold their wings out and let the currents carry them. They rarely flap their wings. This is called soaring. Eagles can stay in the air for long periods of time by soaring.

Birds such as crows, ravens, hawks, and turkey vultures often soar like eagles. You can tell if a bird is an eagle by looking at its size and markings. Use binoculars to do this. Crows and ravens are much smaller than eagles. They also are all black. Hawks are smaller than most adult eagles. Hawks have smaller heads and beaks than eagles. Their tails are longer. Turkey vultures have red heads and white bills. Turkey vultures do

not hold their wings straight out while they soar. They hold their wings in a "V" shape.

Watching Nests

Look up at tree tops for eagle nests. Use binoculars to observe any eagle nests you see. You may even be able to see young eagles in a nest. You are most likely to see young eagles during spring.

Male and female eagles raise their young together. They both hunt and bring food back to the nest for their young. They also teach the young eagles to fly. These young eagles are called fledglings. You may be able to watch fledglings practice flying near their nests.

You may want to come back to any eagle nests you find after several days or weeks. You can see how young eagles change as they grow.

Listening for Eagle Calls

Eagles communicate with loud, high-pitched calls. They use some of these calls to warn

Adult eagles care for their young in nests.

each other of dangers. They use other calls when they mate. Eagles also use calls to communicate with their young.

Listen for eagle calls. You may want to carry a small tape recorder to record eagle calls. Hold the tape recorder into the air while you record eagle calls. Stay very quiet. It may be difficult to make recordings on windy days. The sound of wind can interfere with the sound of eagles' calls.

Recording Your Observations

You may want to record what you see when you observe eagles. Note the times, dates, and places you see eagles. Record the kinds and number of eagles you see. These notes will help you remember your adventure.

You can take photographs of eagles and their environments. Photographs will help you remember exactly how the eagles looked in their environments. You also can draw the eagles you see. You can show your

Eagles use calls to communicate with one another.

photographs and drawings to friends and family members.

Start a bird list if you enjoy watching eagles and other birds. Bird watchers use these lists to keep track of the different birds they see. Use field guides to identify birds you see. Add to the list every time you observe a different bird in its natural surroundings. Note the place and time you see each bird. See how many birds you can add to your list. Many people watch birds all their lives. You may keep your bird list for many years. It will help you remember all the birds you have seen.

You may want to record the eagles you see with a video camera.

North American Field Guide

Bald Eagle

Description: Adult bald eagles have brown bodies, with white heads and tails. They have curved, yellow beaks. Young bald eagles are almost all brown. They may have patches of white on their undersides and tails. Their heads and tails turn white when they are 4 to 5 years of age.

Adult bald eagles measure about 3 feet (.9 meter) from beak to tail. Their wingspans measure from 72 to 90 inches (183 to 229 centimeters). Most adult male bald eagles weigh from 8 to 9 pounds (3.6 to 4.1 kilograms). Most female adult bald eagles weigh from 10 to 14 pounds (4.5 to 6.4 kilograms).

Habitat: Bald eagles usually live near open water. They are common in wooded areas along lakes, rivers, and coastlines. They stay in areas where there is plenty of prey.

Food: Fish, ducks, geese, small mammals

= Range

Golden Eagle

Description: Golden eagles are dark brown, with gold-colored feathers on the backs of their heads and necks. Golden eagles may have patches of white and gold on their wings and bodies. Their curved beaks may be shades of yellow, gray, and black. Adult golden eagles' tails are gray and brown. Young golden eagles' tails may have a patch of white.

Adult golden eagles measure about 3 feet (.9 meter) from beak to tail. Their wingspans measure from 80 to 88 inches (203 to 224 centimeters). Female golden eagles are usually slightly larger than males.

Habitat: Golden eagles often live in areas with hills or mountains. They build their nests in large trees and on cliffs.

Food: Small mammals, snakes, other birds, carrion

= Range

Words to Know

binoculars (buh-NOK-yuh-lurz)—a tool that makes distant objects appear closer

fledgling (FLEJ-ling)—a young bird that is learning to fly

habitat (HAB-uh-tat)—the natural places and conditions in which an animal lives

perch (PURCH)—a resting place for a bird

pesticide (PESS-tuh-side)—a chemical poison used to kill pests such as insects

prey (PRAY)—an animal hunted by another animal for food

range (RAYNJ)—the geographic region where a plant or animal species naturally lives

roost (ROOST)—a place where birds rest and build nests

soar (SOR)—to fly high in the air; eagles soar by riding currents of air without flapping their wings.

talon (TAL-uhn)—a long, sharp claw

To Learn More

National Geographic Society. *Field Guide to the Birds of North America.* Washington: National Geographic Society, 1999.

Patent, Dorothy Hinshaw. *Eagles of America.* New York: Holiday House, 1995.

Potts, Steve. *The Bald Eagle.* Wildlife of North America. Mankato, Minn.: Capstone Press, 1998.

Weidensaul, Scott. *National Audubon Society First Field Guide: Birds.* New York: Scholastic, 1998.

Useful Addresses

Canadian Wildlife Service
Environment Canada
351 St. Joseph Boulevard
Hull, QC K1A 0H3

National Audubon Society
700 Broadway
New York, NY 10003

**National Foundation to Protect
 America's Eagles**
P.O. Box 333
Pigeon Forge, TN 37868

World Center for Birds of Prey
566 West Flying Hawk Lane
Boise, ID 83709

Internet Sites

Canadian Wildlife Service
http://www.cws-scf.ec.gc.ca

The Eagle's Advocate
http://members.aol.com/egladvocat/index.html

**National Foundation to Protect
   America's Eagles**
http://www.eagles.org

The Peregrine Fund
http://www.peregrinefund.org

The Raptor Center
http://www.raptor.cvm.umn.edu

Index